E♭ BARITONE SAXOPHONE

CHRISTMAS FAVORITES

Solos and Band Arrangements
Correlated with Essential Elements Band Method

ARRANGED BY
MICHAEL SWEENEY

Welcome to Essential Elements Christmas Favorites! There are two versions of each holiday selection in this versatile book:
1. The SOLO version (with lyrics) appears on the left-hand page.
2. The FULL BAND arrangement appears on the right-hand page.

Use the optional accompaniment tape when playing solos for friends and family. Your director may also use the accompaniment tape in band rehearsals and concerts.

Solo Pg.	Band Arr. Pg.	Title	Correlated with Essential Elements
2	3	Jingle Bells	Book 1, page 7
4	5	Up On The Housetop	Book 1, page 7
6	7	The Hanukkah Song	Book 1, page 19
8	9	A Holly Jolly Christmas	Book 1, page 21
10	11	We Wish You A Merry Christmas	Book 1, page 21
12	13	Frosty The Snow Man	Book 1, page 25
14	15	Rockin' Around The Christmas Tree	Book 1, page 25
16	17	Jingle-Bell Rock	Book 2, page 8
18	19	Rudolph The Red-Nosed Reindeer	Book 2, page 8
20	21	Let It Snow! Let It Snow! Let It Snow!	Book 2, page 8
22	23	The Christmas Song	Book 2, page 29

ISBN 978-0-7935-1759-6

HAL•LEONARD® CORPORATION
7777 W. BLUEMOUND RD. P.O. BOX 13819 MILWAUKEE, WI 53213

Copyright © 1992 HAL LEONARD PUBLISHING CORPORATION
International Copyright Secured   All Rights Reserved

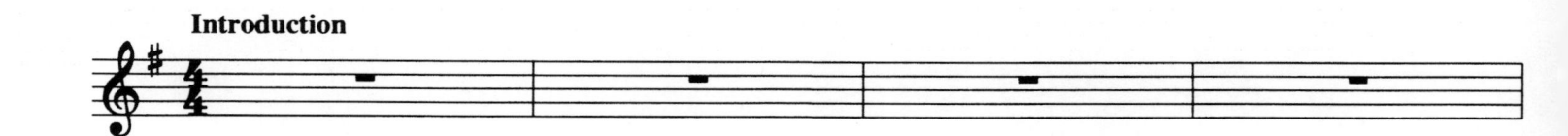

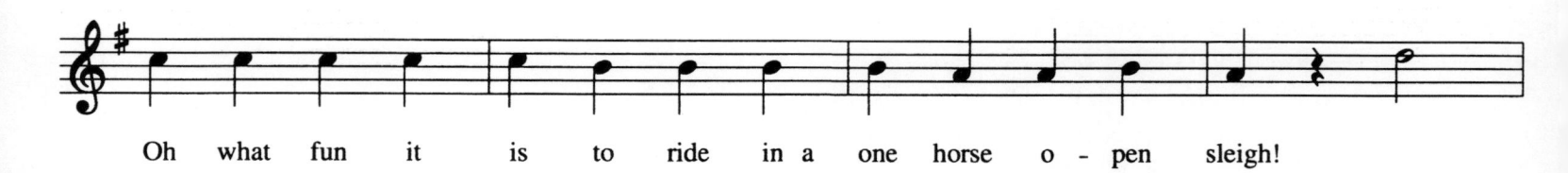

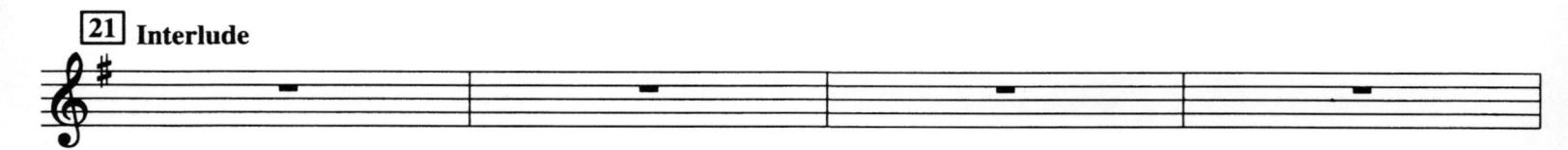

JINGLE BELLS

Words and Music by J. PIERPONT
Arranged by MICHAEL SWEENEY

Solo

Introduction

5
Jin - gle Bells, Jin - gle Bells, Jin - gle all the way.

Oh what fun it is to ride in a one horse o - pen sleigh!

13
Jin - gle Bells, Jin - gle Bells, Jin - gle all the way.

Oh what fun it is to ride in a one horse o - pen sleigh!

21 **Interlude**

Oh what fun it is to ride in a one horse o - pen sleigh!

00862508

Copyright © 1992 HAL LEONARD PUBLISHING CORPORATION
International Copyright Secured   All Rights Reserved

JINGLE BELLS

Band Arrangement

Words and Music by J. PIERPONT
Arranged by MICHAEL SWEENEY

UP ON THE HOUSETOP

Arranged by MICHAEL SWEENEY

Solo

Introduction

Up on the house-top reindeer pause, Out jumps good old Santa Claus; Down through the chimney with lots of toys, All for the little ones, Christmas joys. Ho, ho, ho! Who wouldn't go! Ho, ho, ho! Who wouldn't go! Up on the house-top, click, click, click, Down through the chimney with good Saint Nick.

00862508

Copyright © 1992 HAL LEONARD PUBLISHING CORPORATION
International Copyright Secured   All Rights Reserved

UP ON THE HOUSETOP

Band Arrangement

Arranged by MICHAEL SWEENEY

THE HANUKKAH SONG

Arranged by MICHAEL SWEENEY

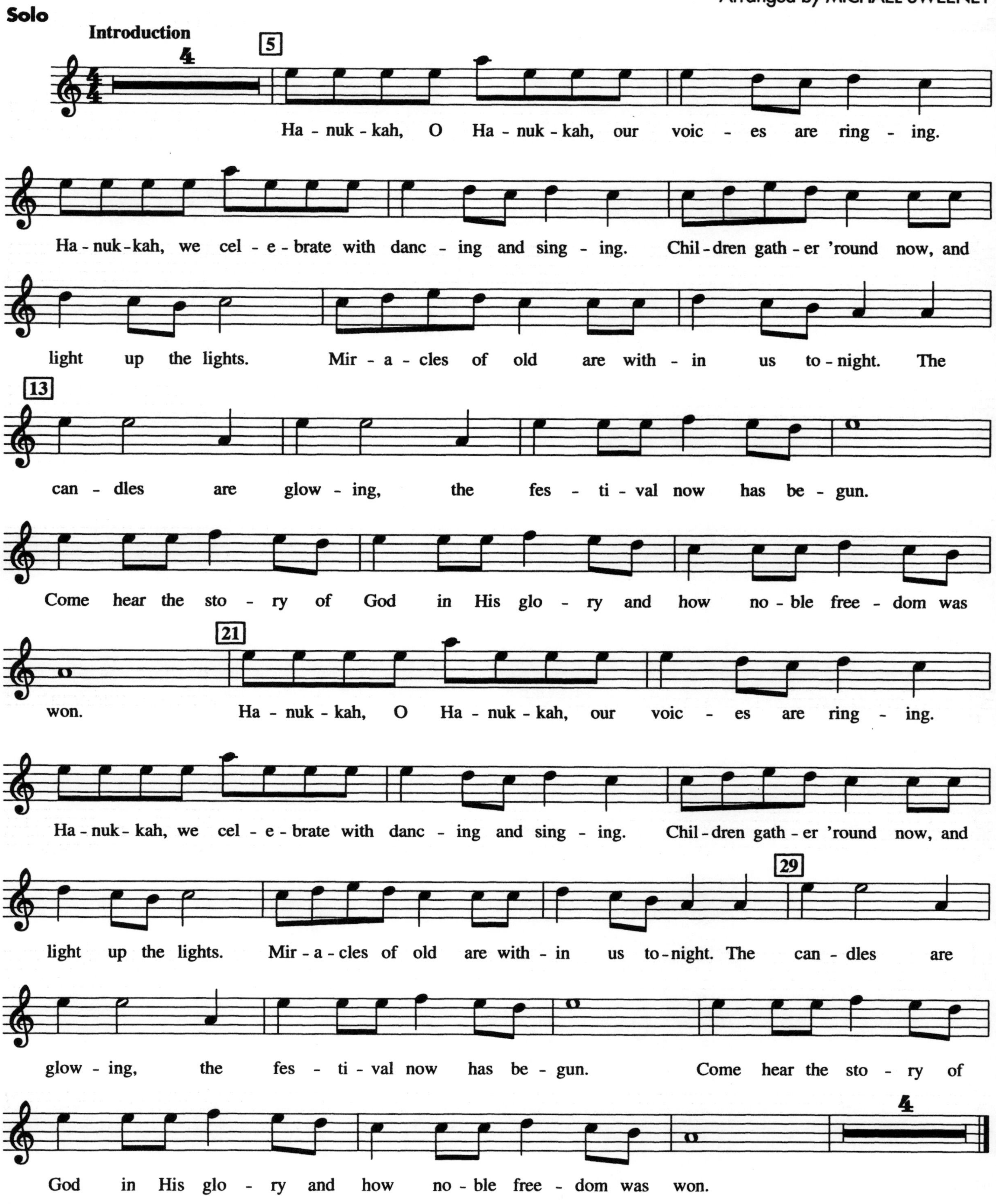

00862508

THE HANUKKAH SONG

Band Arrangement

Arranged by MICHAEL SWEENEY

A Holly Jolly Christmas

Music and Lyrics by JOHNNY MARKS
Arranged by MICHAEL SWEENEY

WE WISH YOU A MERRY CHRISTMAS

Solo

Arranged by MICHAEL SWEENEY

00862508

WE WISH YOU A MERRY CHRISTMAS

Band Arrangement

Arranged by MICHAEL SWEENEY

00862508

FROSTY THE SNOW MAN

Words and Music by STEVE NELSON and JACK ROLLINS
Arranged by MICHAEL SWEENEY

Solo

00862508

Frosty the Snow Man

Band Arrangement

Words and Music by STEVE NELSON and JACK ROLLINS
Arranged by MICHAEL SWEENEY

ROCKIN' AROUND THE CHRISTMAS TREE

Music and Lyrics by JOHNNY MARKS
Arranged by MICHAEL SWEENEY

Solo

Rock-in' a-round the Christ-mas tree __ at the Christ-mas par-ty
Rock-in' a-round the Christ-mas tree __ let the Christ-mas spir-it
hop. Mis-tle-toe hung where you can see __ ev-'ry cou-ple tries to
ring. Lat-er we'll have some pump-kin pie __ and we'll
stop. do some car-ol-ing. You will get a sen-ti-men-tal feel-ing when you
hear voic-es sing-ing, "Let's be jol-ly, Deck the halls with
boughs of hol-ly." Rock-in' a-round the Christ-mas tree. __ Have a
hap-py hol-i-day. Ev-'ry-one danc-ing mer-ri-ly __ in the
new old fash-ioned way. Rock-in' a-round the Christ-mas tree. __ Have a
hap-py hol-i-day. Ev-'ry-one danc-ing mer-ri-ly __ in the
new old fash-ioned way. __

00862508

Copyright © 1958, Renewed 1986 St. Nicholas Music, Inc., 1619 Broadway, New York, New York 10019
This arrangement Copyright © 1992 St. Nicholas Music, Inc.
All Rights Reserved

ROCKIN' AROUND THE CHRISTMAS TREE

Music and Lyrics by **JOHNNY MARKS**
Arranged by MICHAEL SWEENEY

Band Arrangement

00862508

JINGLE-BELL ROCK

Words and Music by JOE BEAL and JIM BOOTHE
Arranged by MICHAEL SWEENEY

Solo

Jin-gle-bell, Jin-gle-bell, Jin-gle-bell rock Jin-gle-bell swing and Jin-gle-bells ring. Snow-in' and blow-in' up bush-els of fun Now the Jin-gle-hop has be-gun. Jin-gle-bell, Jin-gle-bell, Jin-gle-bell rock Jin-gle-bells chime in Jin-gle-bell time. Danc-in' and pranc-in' in Jin-gle-bell Square In the frost-y air. What a bright time, it's the right time to rock the night a-way. Jin-gle-bell time is a swell time to go glid-in' in a one-horse sleigh. Gid-dy-ap, Jin-gle-horse pick up your feet. Jin-gle a-round the clock. Mix and min-gle in a jin-gl-in' beat. That's the Jin-gle-bell, That's the Jin-gle-bell, That's the Jin-gle-bell rock.

00862508

Copyright © 1957 (Renewed) by Cornell Music, Inc.
All Rights controlled by Chappell & Co. (Intersong Music, Publisher)
This arrangement Copyright © 1992 by Chappell & Co.
International Copyright Secured   All Rights Reserved

RUDOLPH THE RED-NOSED REINDEER

Music and Lyrics by JOHNNY MARKS
Arranged by MICHAEL SWEENEY

Solo

00862508

Rudolph the Red-Nosed Reindeer

Band Arrangement

Music and Lyrics by JOHNNY MARKS
Arranged by MICHAEL SWEENEY

00862508

Copyright © 1949, Renewed 1977 St. Nicholas Music, Inc., 1619 Broadway, New York, New York 10019
This arrangement Copyright © 1992 by St. Nicholas Music, Inc.
All Rights Reserved

LET IT SNOW! LET IT SNOW! LET IT SNOW!

Words by SAMMY CAHN
Music by JULE STYNE
Arranged by MICHAEL SWEENEY

Solo

00862508

LET IT SNOW! LET IT SNOW! LET IT SNOW!

Band Arrangement

Words by SAMMY CAHN
Music by JULE STYNE
Arranged by MICHAEL SWEENEY

THE CHRISTMAS SONG

Music and Lyric by MEL TORME and ROBERT WELLS
Arranged by MICHAEL SWEENEY

THE CHRISTMAS SONG

Band Arrangement

Music and Lyric by MEL TORME and ROBERT WELLS
Arranged by MICHAEL SWEENEY

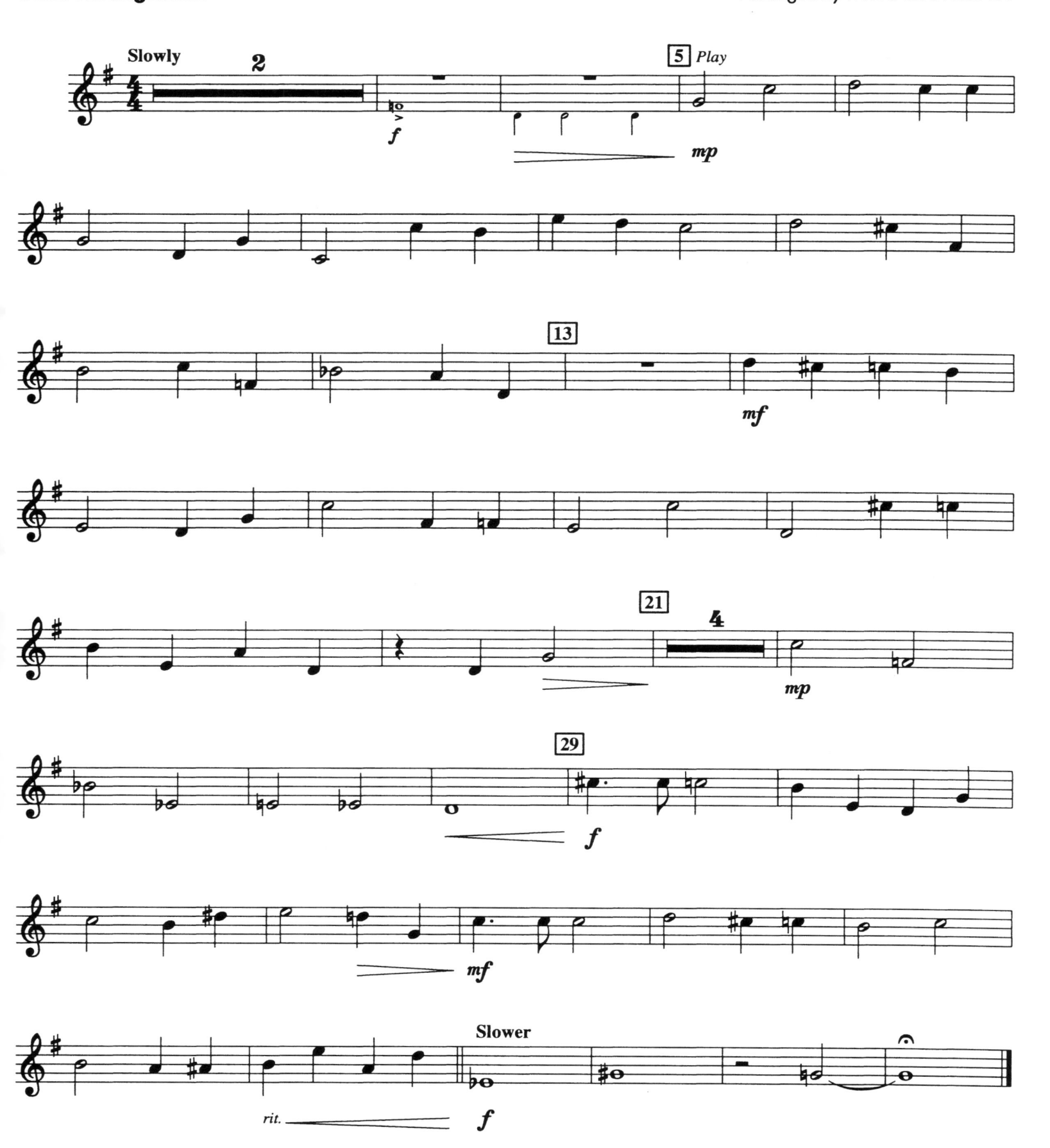

00862508

© 1946, 1992 EDWIN H. MORRIS & COMPANY, A Division of MPL Communications, Inc.
© Renewed 1974 EDWIN H. MORRIS & COMPANY, A Division of MPL Communications, Inc.
International Copyright Secured   All Rights Reserved